CW00821225

CLASSIC MARQUES

The Reliant Three-Wheeler
1973-2002

ELVIS PAYNE AND STUART CYPHUS

NOSTALGIA ROAD

First published by Crécy Publishing Ltd 2012

© Text: Nostalgia Road 2012
© Photographs: As credited

All rights reserved. No part of this book may be reproduced or transmitted in any form or by any means electronic or mechanical, including photocopying, recording or by any information storage without permission from the Publisher in writing. All enquiries should be directed to the Publisher.

A CIP record for this book is available from the British Library

ISBN 9 781908 347060

Front Cover: The final Reliant: the Robin 65, built to mark the 65th anniversary of the foundation of the Reliant Motor Company, also marked the end of vehicle production in Staffordshire. As befitted the name, 65 examples were produced with the last car leaving the factory on 14 February 2001.

Rear Cover Top: For technical interest, Reliant created a fullsized and fully-drivable cutaway Robin in order to demonstrate just how compact a vehicle the Robin really was. This view clearly demonstrates how the chassis rose up at the front to clear the front wheel and also contributed to impact protection.

Rear Cover Bottom: The Robin was styled to appeal to a mass audience, including existing owners of four-wheeled vehicles. Publicity shots of families picnicking helped to demonstrate the notion that this was potentially an option as a second car suitable for the whole family, with the innovative opening rear window once more to the fore.

Contents Page: After Reliant announced in 2000 that it was no longer to make three-wheelers, it carried on producing the Robin LX, SLX, and the B.R.G and Royale — as pictured here — models during the run down.

All the illustrations, unless otherwise indicated, are from Elvis Payne's collection or have been supplied to him by Derick Smith, Kerry Croxton or Thomas Touw.

Printed in Malta by Melita Press

Crécy Publishing Limited
1a Ringway Trading Estate
Shadowmoss Road
Manchester M22 5LH

www.crecy.co.uk

CONTENTS

Introduction

This book follows on from *The Reliant Three-Wheeler 1935-1973*, published in 2011, and takes the Reliant story on from October 1973. The post-1973 Reliants hold great memories for me and it was partly those and my interest in the Reliant Motor Company that led to the creation of my web site at www.3-wheelers.com. Whilst my current Reliant is now a 1961 Reliant Mk VI 5cwt van, my first Reliant was a 1973 Super Robin followed a few years later by a 1982 Rialto (and then a few more Reliants). As my daily transport during my university years and beyond, the Robin was the car that hurtled through the darkness along winding country roads with my sister, Sharron, on board heading to the maternity ward at Burton-on-Trent hospital when she was about to give birth. It was also the vehicle that had me laughing for a week when the front tyre blew out and a fellow passenger screamed for her life and suddenly adopted the crash position. The vehicle itself just pulled up in a straight line with no harm done. Revenge, however, was swift when, just a few weeks later, the Robin broke down and, after a phone call to my parents, my dad (John) scared me silly towing me home behind his Vauxhall Cavalier at 60mph — something he then laughed at for a week. I could go on (and on) but my memoirs are not the topic of this book.

My thanks go to fellow co-author Stuart Cyphus whose original manuscript formed the basis for this book when an editorial decision was made to split the Reliant story into two volumes. Our sincere thanks also go to Jonathan Heynes for providing so much of his time creating a unique chapter on Reliant history exclusively for this book. Thanks also go to Tamworth Library for allowing me access to old copies of the *Tamworth Herald* and to members of the R3W Reliant forum (www.r3w.co.uk) and the Reliant Owners Club (www.reliantownersclub.co.uk) for filling in various gaps of information. Most of the images in this book come from my own collection though supplemented with additional photographs and information from David Poole, Kerry Croxton, Mark and Sue Cropper, Martin North, Susan Nelson and Thomas Touw. I would like to dedicate this volume not only to my wife Caroline and son Harvey who both continually make me smile and remain patient concerning all things Reliant but also to my sister and her fiancé, Adam Pelham, who no matter how busy, are always there for my mum Kath on a day-to-day basis.

Elvis Payne,
Tamworth, July 2011

As we pick up the Reliant story in October 1973 upon the introduction of the Reliant Robin from the ashes of the Regal's long reign, we see a company at the very height of its success, but, as the Robin made its bow, the cracks were already starting to appear in an otherwise glittering facade. The latter years at Tamworth, set against a national backdrop of ever-worsening labour relations, political battles and financial recessions throughout the late 1970s and into the early 1980s, are a prime case study for the student of economics to show how a highly successful company could be felled so rapidly. It is, therefore, surprising that, despite their fame (or notoriety), there has been no major account of the later Reliant vehicles placed in print until now. This oversight is all the more surprising considering there can be few people around today who cannot recognise a post-1973 Reliant three-wheeler. (Although whether or not they can correctly name the exact model, or even place the make and model names in their correct order, is usually another matter entirely.)

As work commenced on this volume it became clear that there is, indeed, something of a truism in the apparent contradiction that it is often easier to find details of events or vehicles of almost a century ago than to find details of happenings in more recent decades. That certainly proved to be the case with the Reliant three-wheeler. Here I extend my thanks, once more, to my co-author Elvis Payne, who again stepped into the breech without so much as a moment's hesitation. Meanwhile, I also thank Daniel Rodd, one of the enthusiastic younger generation of Reliant enthusiasts who are doing so much to keep the legend alive far into the future. It was a long mid-summer afternoon spent in his company along with his piles of paper and his award-winning 1986 Reliant Rialto 2 estate that did much to unravel some of the complexities of the Reliant three-wheeler's later years. Now, as Elvis and I sign off this second volume of the Reliant three-wheeler story, we trust we have done justice, both to our memories and to the cars themselves.

Stuart Cyphus,
Oxford, July 2011

Left: Elvis Payne's old 1982 Rialto guarded by swans at Burslem Park in Stoke-on-Trent. It was purchased in 1993 whilst at university for £875 — an absolute fortune at the time given the size of student loans but worth its weight in gold when it rained.

Right: After many and varied exploits in the 1980s with a near legendary Regal 3/30, Stuart Cyphus' family made one last excursion into Reliant motoring in 2001 with this 1983 Rialto GLS saloon. Like all Reliants, this car quickly proved it had a strong personality all of its own, being particularly fond of dropping its boot lid open with no warning given, more often than not whilst on the move!

The Robin Takes Flight: 1973-1981

During the early 1970s, the Reliant Motor Company was at the very height of its success, with turnover constantly averaging over £20,000,000 per year. Its three-wheeler range was without competition in the home market and export sales of Reliant vehicles were raking money in from all around the world. After 20 years of dominating the British three-wheeler market, the Reliant Regal finally ceased production on 31 October 1973. Earlier in the month, the first examples of its much-anticipated replacement had begun their journey down the Two Gates' production line. Unveiled to an eager public on 2 October, Ray Wiggin, Reliant's Managing Director, announced to the press that, 'This is the car you've all asked for' — the Reliant Robin. Reliant had invested more than £1 million in new buildings and equipment to produce the Robin, resulting in dramatic changes to its sites at Two Gates, Shenstone and Kettlebrook. At the Kettlebrook plant alone, the entire internal organisation was changed in July 1973, during the fortnight holiday, and workers came back to start producing bodies in a totally new fashion with the introduction of hot press moulding. With such changes taking place the local *Tamworth Herald* quoted Ray Wiggin as saying, 'We now have Europe's largest and most modern plant for vehicles of this type, with by far the largest capacity outside of the United States.'

A 1967 film on Reliant exports shows the hand of Ray Wiggin with a model of the next generation of Reliant three-wheelers. The similarities between the model and what would become the Reliant Robin are instantly recognisable.

This general view of the Two Gates factory grounds, taken on 18 December 1972, is important for having captured a pre-production Robin van standing in the yard almost an entire year before the model would make its public bow. Bearing a registration number that appears to be NRF 502L, this is possibly the earliest known view of a completed Reliant Robin.

Reliant invested heavily on the south side of its Two Gates premises, building four large buildings, two of which were to incorporate the assembly lines for the Robin. This looks to be building No 1, which was the body storage area and also incorporated the Robin Paint and Chassis Assembly shops. *David Poole*

It's October 1973 and the brand-new high-level assembly line for the Robin range swings into action. This new line operated on the conveyor belt principle with the tracks continually moving, a far cry from earlier years when each car had to be manually pushed along the line. *Thomas Touw*

The Robin saloon and van range was an entirely new design from the ground up, with a wider, simpler and considerably lighter chassis naturally owing more to the Bond Bug than to the Regal, hardly surprising considering both were designed by Ogle Designs Ltd. That said, Ogle's Tom Karen announced that the Bug and the Robin, whilst sharing the same engineering philosophy, were totally different in concept. The Bond Bug was aimed at the 17-24 age group for young people who wanted a fun sports car whilst the Robin was to attract people who drove conventional saloon and estate cars as well as motorcycles. For that reason he described the Robin as a 'prettier vehicle than the bug'. To help the Robin appeal to both feminine and masculine taste, a range of eight new colours were introduced; these included the somewhat dazzling Carnival Pink. The all-important appearance was a great deal more rounded and modern in shape than the preceding Regal 3/25-3/30, the Robin actually having more of a 'family' link to the long-gone Regal Mark VI of 13 years earlier!

Before any fibreglass-bodied vehicle can enter production, a full sized mock-up of the body shell has first to be created from which the all-important moulds can be taken.

A new Robin freshly hatched from its shell. The various individual sections that created the body were all assembled together to form a single master mould in which an outer layer of gelcoat was applied and then the fibreglass matting was applied by hand. Twenty-four hours later, the fibreglass had cured, enabling the jigs to be taken apart revealing a new-born Reliant. *David Poole*

Below: Like any other vehicle, the Robin underwent compulsory stress and crash testing at the Motor Industry Research Association (MIRA) testing facilities in Warwickshire prior to its public debut. With its strong steel chassis and impact absorbing fibreglass body, the Reliant three-wheeler always achieved high marks in such tests.

Top Left: The traditional hand-laying of fibreglass was both a time and a labour-intensive activity. With the Robin came new techniques to speed up the manufacturing of doors and bonnets with the introduction of hot press moulding using a 1,000ton press. *David Poole*

Middle Left: With the new hot press moulding technique in operation, a number of tests were done to ensure the optimal thickness that a door needed to be to have enough strength. This development model shows one door that has failed. *David Poole*

Below: A 1974 Reliant Robin in perhaps the most flamboyant and controversial colour ever offered by Reliant — the very bright Carnival Pink. Listed for only one single year, Carnival Pink is perhaps the rarest of all Reliant colours.

Below: The cover of the 1973 launch brochure, proudly proclaiming the Robin as 'a new idea from the ground up' though the car photographed was pre-production car number four and featured a number of details not present in the production version, most notably a petrol cap set much higher than expected.

Robin

A new idea from the ground up

Images in Reliant brochures were always designed to show the vehicle or its attributes to best effect. This particular shot, again found in the 1973 launch brochure, is somewhat unrealistic as it depicts a male driver actually stopping and asking a *lady* for directions!

The interior of the Robin was completely modernised over the outgoing Regal with numerous clocks, modern switches, including indicator and horn switches, attached to the steering column and, for the first time in a Reliant, a radio that came as an optional extra for £33.36 (inc VAT).

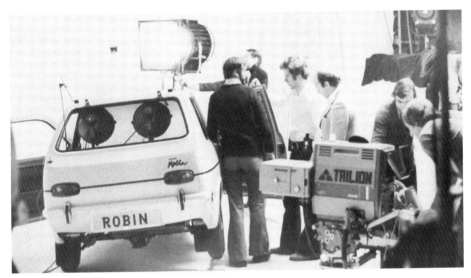

The Robin at Halliford Studios in Shepperton set to make its television debut for a 30sec commercial. Produced by the Allardyce Agency for Reliant, the theme of the commercial was 'Let's invent the economy car'. The adverts were shown in 1973 on 10 ITV channels covering 85% of the UK. *Thomas Touw*

The Robin van had a payload of 5cwt and offered many small businesses an economical workhorse. In its most basic form, it could be purchased unpainted with a primer finish and no passenger seat. (The passenger seat was an optional extra for £14.85.)

Power for the Robin came, not unexpectedly, from the recently introduced 32bhp 748cc all-aluminium engine, which provided power to the rear wheels through a four-speed gearbox that now had synchromesh on all four gears. Modern 10in road wheels were fitted, again the result of lessons learned with the Bug, and took the projected top speed to just over 80mph. Overall dimensions were a length of 10ft 11in, a width of 4ft 8in and a height of 4ft 6in, with the wheelbase being 7ft 1in and rear track being 4ft 1in. However, unlike the later model Regals, the Robin had no external boot compartment. Instead the luggage area was located behind the rear seat with access being through the lift-up rear window allowing a loading space of 30cu ft with the rear seats folded down. In effect, the Reliant Robin was a pioneer of the 'hatchback' craze that was poised to sweep the motor industry, but, in 1973, the word was virtually unknown, and so, with a folding rear seat also on the specification list, the Robin was billed as an 'economy saloon-estate' in its contemporary advertising. Two variants of the Robin saloon and van were offered at the launch, these being the standard Robin priced at £779.35 including VAT (£677.05 for the Robin Van) and the Super Robin priced at £826.42 including VAT (£737.00 for the Super Robin Van).

Elsewhere in the three-wheeler range, both the Bond Bug and the Reliant TW9 were to gain the 748cc engine during October 1973, with the Bug accordingly renamed as the 750ES but, as 1973 gave way to 1974, it was the Robin that continued to hold centre-stage. By February 1974, just three months after its launch, sales were already approaching the 6,000 mark with the top-of-the-range Super Robin accounting for around 60% of the demand. With the Robin in such a strong position and with so little production line capacity available at Two Gates, something clearly had to give. As a consequence, during May 1974, production of both the four-wheeled Rebel and Bug models were suspended in an effort to free some valuable space for the ever-increasing Robin line. Indeed, by the end of September 1974, the 10,000th Robin had been sold, along with the setting of a new production record of no less than 330 vehicles a week coming off the line.

The Robin was further boosted by its connections with royalty. On 15 July 1975 HRH Princess Anne visited Reliant and spent five hours visiting all three sites: Two Gates, Kettlebrook and Shenstone. Princess Anne arrived at Reliant, having driven herself there in her Reliant Scimitar GTE sports car, and, whilst talking to employees, she spoke openly about the Tropic Green Robin Saloon she also owned and had learnt to drive in.

Although the Robin was breaking all records for Reliant, the company was forever looking to the future, as proved in October 1975, when the basic 748cc engine was bored out to 848cc and the carburettor changed from a Zenith downdraft to a SU carburettor increasing power from 32 to 40bhp. From this point on, the Robin range received an '850' suffix to its name and a few additional tweaks, such as a higher fuel filler, for it had been found that on 750cc cars, the fuel filler cap had been set too low and in some circumstances, petrol could escape from the cap on sharp corners.

For technical interest, Reliant created a full-sized and fully-drivable cutaway Robin in order to demonstrate just how compact a vehicle the Robin really was. This view clearly demonstrates how the chassis rose up at the front to clear the front wheel and also contributed to impact protection.

Despite gaining the Robin's 748cc engine in October 1973 to create the new 750E and 750ES models, demand for the Bug was starting to fade and, in May 1974, the decision was taken to halt production in order to free valuable capacity on the production line for the Robin. *Thomas Touw*

13

Introducing

Robin

best thing since the mini

Robin is an *economy-saloon-estate* — first of its kind, the most practical small car on the roads of Britain today.
    Saloon because it has 4 seats and a boot. Estate because you can open up the big back window like a door, reach in and fold down the back seat. In that instant you have *thirty cubic feet* of loadspace.
    Economy because its lively 750 cc engine gives you up to 60 mpg and there's only £10 road tax. Add to that a body that never rusts — and what have you got?
    A collection of advantages that no other car can match.
    And doesn't it look good?

For its time the Robin was unique in that it was a hatchback. Its arrival and importance were compared with those of the Austin Mini and Reliant jokingly warned Longbridge to 'watch out'. It is somewhat ironic that Reliant advertised the Robin as 'the best thing since the mini', for the Mini had been instigated in 1956 by Leonard Lord, the head of BMC because of his hatred of all 'bubblecars' and three-wheelers, hoping to clear the streets of such vehicles.

Into 1977, and the UK was riding high on the crest of a patriotic wave, for this was the year of the Silver Jubilee of HM Queen Elizabeth II. The Reliant Motor Company celebrated the occasion in style with the 'Jubilee' Robin Super 850, of which only 750 were produced, each with a special bonnet badge bearing the car's individual number. Painted in Royal Red, the Jubilee Robin had silver coach lining, a silver name style, plus 'Jubilee' insignia etched on the rear window and on the hubs of the alloy rear wheels. Inside the car was to be found silver/grey upholstery with matching carpets and headlining. Mechanically there were no changes. The Jubilee Robin went on sale just before the Queen's official jubilee celebrations in July 1977 with the batch of 750 being split between 200 dealers, and all were sold within a few short weeks, with one dealer reporting that he had sold his entire allocation of cars before he'd even finished putting up the promotional posters in the showroom.

Perhaps one of the most important things this image captures is not Robins being sanded before entering the paint shop but the camaraderie amongst the company's employees. People enjoyed working for Reliant and very few chose to leave. *Thomas Touw*

The 1974 fuel crisis resulted in George W. Bentley Ltd, refrigeration specialist of Havant, Hampshire replacing its existing service vehicle with a Robin van. Once decorated with orange and white livery, the vehicle proved to be so eye-catching with the general public that a second example was ordered. *Thomas Touw*

Despite the public appearance of a company still at the peak of its game and able to sell everything it made, behind the scenes, all was far from well at Tamworth as the second half of the 1970s progressed. To make matters worse for those who recognised the signs, neither of the events that are now to be recounted were directly the fault of Reliant yet the company was to be powerless against the fallout from them. On the wider British vehicle scene, ever since the mid-1960s there had been endless witch-hunts and newspaper campaigns against the humble National Health Service invalid tricycle — those small, pale blue, single-seat three-wheelers instantly recognisable to an entire generation as the main means of transport for the nation's disabled persons. A number of such tricycles were undergoing crash testing and safety trials, first at the Cranfield Institute of Technology and then at the Motor Industry Research Association (MIRA). The results were utterly damning and did much to hasten the final demise of the British invalid tricycle in 1976 and, of course, the press had a field day with the very public fall of the invalid tricycle industry. Although the invalid tricycle was the main target, the Reliant three-wheeler found itself dangerously close to the resulting negative fallout as the press were now never missing an opportunity to publish lurid horror stories regarding the safety and stability of *any* three-wheeled vehicle and were none too fussed about letting trifling matters such as the truth get in the way of a good story. The British public swallowed the stories hook, line and sinker, and slowly, sales of the Reliant three-wheeler began to be affected as the decade wore on.

Reliant was host to a number of famous faces throughout the years with perhaps the most notable being Princess Anne, seen here with Ray Wiggin in July 1975 on the Robin assembly line. For co-author Elvis Payne the most important person in this photo is, perhaps, the chap on the left-hand side with the beard — for this is his Father-in-Law, Barry Stokes, who worked for Reliant during the 1970s. *David Poole*

INTRODUCING THE 70mpg CAR.

Brighter performance, greater economy. That's the amazing new Robin 850.

We've given the Robin a new bigger 850cc aluminium engine. So it's quicker off the mark with a lively performance ideal for town driving.

But here's the remarkable thing. Because of the engine efficiency there's no loss of famous Robin economy.

In fact, it's increased.

Test figures show over 60mpg at a constant 50mph and over 70mpg at 40mph.

But petrol isn't the only economy. The body is glassfibre. It can't rust. You save a garage. And it keeps its resale value.

Road Tax is only £16 a year instead of the normal £40.

So much for cheaper motoring. Look what else the Robin 850 offers. The improved suspension makes for a smooth, more comfortable ride. It is easy to park. With room for 4 adults. And 8½ cubic feet of luggage space. A staggering 30 cubic feet with the back seat down.

If you're looking for bright performance and great economy introduce yourself to the new Robin 850.

Get a test drive today.

To: Marketing Services, Reliant Motor Company Limited, Tamworth, Staffordshire B77 1HN. Or phone Tamworth (0827) 69595 any time.

Please send me details of:
☐ Robin Saloons for £XXXX ☐ Robin Vans from £XXXX
☐ Tick here if you would like a test drive.

Name _____

Address _____

_____ Age if under 18 _____

Prices are ex works and include VAT and car tax.

In October 1975 the Reliant Robin 850 was announced in a blaze of publicity, the larger engine allowing the Robin to reach over 80mph and to return 70mpg fuel consumption. Interestingly, the car shown in this particular advertisement is in fact an air-brushed 748cc car. The give-away? Note the low position of the fuel filler cap.

The Robin 850 was easily able to exceed 80mph making it more than capable of keeping up with motorway speeds.

Reliant took the Robin to numerous locations like this harbour scene to try and photograph it in such a way that it showed the Robin as something more than just a vehicle for economy motoring. *Thomas Touw*

A number of 850cc engines receive a final inspection on the production line prior to being mounted in the Robin. *Thomas Touw*

The new 850cc engine fitted to the Robin meant that it could do the benchmark 0 to 60mph in 16.1sec. Not enough to set the tarmac on fire but, in the 1970s, a fairly respectable figure and on a par with quite a few four-wheelers.

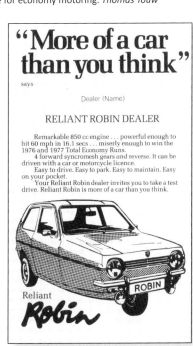

"More of a car than you think"

says

Dealer (Name)

RELIANT ROBIN DEALER

Remarkable 850 cc engine . . . powerful enough to hit 60 mph in 16.1 secs . . . miserly enough to win the 1976 and 1977 Total Economy Runs.

4 forward syncromesh gears and reverse. It can be driven with a car or motorcycle licence.

Easy to drive. Easy to park. Easy to maintain. Easy on your pocket.

Your Reliant Robin dealer invites you to take a test drive. Reliant Robin is more of a car than you think.

Reliant
Robin

ROBIN

17

The Robin was styled to appeal to a mass audience, including existing owners of four-wheeled vehicles. Publicity shots of families picnicking helped to demonstrate the notion that this was potentially an option as a second car suitable for the whole family, with the innovative opening rear window once more to the fore.

In *The Reliant Three-Wheeler 1935-1973* (published in 2011), Two Strokes Ltd of Church Road, Stanmore, Middlesex, was discussed for its unique range of special Reliant models, the most famous of which was the Supervan-based TS Safari. Although not as aesthetically pleasing as the original, the firm also produced a Robin 850-based Safari in 1975 complete with customary black roof, amber roof window and rear air vents. Sadly, very few were sold. *Kerry Croxton*

The Reliant Robin Super 850 estate car was a welcome addition to the range in March 1976. Originally intended to be produced only in limited numbers, public demand soon proved otherwise and, from 1977 until the end of Robin production in October 1981, the estate would consistently top Reliant's sales graphs.

During the course of its October 1973 road test of the new Reliant three-wheeler, *Motor* magazine's photographer unwittingly managed to capture in the same frame a prime example of a National Health Service invalid tricycle, then one of the most vilified vehicles on the road.

Meanwhile, the Reliant Motor Company was also coming under attack from the inside as time went on. Although the company had been fortunate in enjoying excellent worker/management relations since its very beginnings, by the late 1960s UK industry as a whole became embroiled in a prolonged and extremely bitter power struggle between the government and the unions, which grew steadily worse as the years went on. By the mid-1970s, strikes were threatening to paralyse the country and the Reliant Motor Company was not immune as most of their workers were affiliated to the Trade & General Workers Union (TGWU), one of the largest and most militant unions of its

The limited edition Robin Jubilee model helped to celebrate the Silver Jubilee of HM Queen Elizabeth II in 1977.

In 1975 sales of the Robin were boosted in Austria when the government passed new legislation that allowed a motorcyclist to pass the motorcycle test in a three-wheeler. By the end of that year a great number of the 250 left-hand Robins that had been imported to Austria had been sold to 12 driving schools. *Thomas Touw*

era. As a result, the Tamworth production lines were often stationary, sometimes for weeks on end as the TGWU fought out its national grievances. By early 1977, such strikes are believed to have cost Reliant £1 million in lost production, further underlined by the company recording a trading loss of £899,000 for the 1976/77 financial year, forcing the laying-off of 650 workers. Not even the Robin's impressive sales figures between 1973 and 1976 were enough to lift the financial gloom and, in July 1977, the Hodge Group, owners of the Reliant Motor Company, voted to sell a 76% controlling interest in Reliant to J. F. Nash Securities Ltd.

In many ways, J. F. Nash Securities had much the same designs on the Reliant Motor Company as the Hodge Group had exhibited back in 1962, with the new owners wishing to expand the industrial interests within its commercial and financial portfolio. Immediately upon assuming command, J. F. Nash Ltd, now operating simply as 'the Nash Group', turned its attention to clearing out some of the slower-selling lines of the Reliant Motor Company in a bid to 'restructure the

Opposite: It was not only large organisations that found numerous uses for the TW9 but also local companies as well. From 1973 until 1977, when production rights were sold to BTB Engineering of Lancashire, the UK-market TW9 would receive periodic mechanical upgrades in line with other Reliant models, gaining the 748cc engine in October 1973 and then the 848cc version in 1975.

20

The TW9 was such a versatile model that it continued to be made well into the Robin years, especially after Reliant discovered that there was also a lucrative market for it in the UK as well as abroad.

size and organisation of the company' as an early press release put it. The Reliant TW9 16cwt pick-up was no longer bringing in quite as much money, pound-for-pound, as it had done in the late 1960s and so, towards the end of 1977, the production rights to the TW9 in the UK was sold off to BTB Engineering Ltd of Blackburn, Lancashire, who, coincidentally, had been producing their own range of TW9-based vehicles since October 1975. BTB Engineering were now able to do as it pleased and chose to rename the Reliant TW9 as the BTB Ant, with UK production continuing at a very low rate until May 1987. Back at Tamworth, the coming of the Nash organisation also heralded the departure of Ray Wiggin, the driving force behind most of the Reliant company's success, who resigned his position of Managing Director 'for personal reasons' and severed connections with the company in October 1977, going on to establish his own business at Lichfield.

The late 1970s were a bleak time for Reliant, which now had to fight to survive. The company reported losses for 1976 through to 1978, making a loss in that year alone of £152,639 despite a turnover of £20 million. Things were not helped with the recall of the Robin following issues with many early cars suffering from the steering box shearing from its mounting points, rendering the steering useless at high speeds, a potentially lethal issue cured by the introduction of a 'strut and cradle' bracket effectively to wedge the steering box against the top chassis rail in case of fracture! By December 1979 25,000 Robins had been recalled and modified, something Reliant's new Managing Director, 36-year-old Ritchie Spencer, termed as 'a foul and depressing business'. However, despite this and a National Engineering strike in 1979 that affected many of Reliant's suppliers, sales of the Robin were healthy and by the end of the year the company was able to report a modest profit of £249,441.

The Robin 850 assembly line in the late 1970s, the sheer volume of vehicles being produced at this time is evident. *Thomas Touw*

A year after the very successful 'Jubilee' special edition cars, Reliant again took advantage of such marketing ploys with the 1978 Robin GBS (Great Britain Special). Available only in white with red and blue decals plus a Tartan pattern to the interior, some 400 GBSs were sold between 1978 and 1981.

Decline and Fall: 1981-1995

The 1980s started badly with a severe recession and, by the end of 1981, Reliant recorded a trading loss of £1,054,291 a fact not helped by £624,132 being paid out in redundancy payments as the Nash Group's reduction of Reliant's diversity began to bite. By now the Robin range had been in production for almost seven years but despite its losses, Reliant had still been investing in new vehicles to meet the changing tastes of the early 1980s. Accordingly, the Robin gave way to its successor in October 1981 as the production lines were given over to the new Reliant Rialto, although this model's official announcement would not be made until 13 January 1982. Consisting of a saloon, an estate and a 5-cwt van, the Rialto range was practically identical mechanically to the outgoing Robin 850, utilising the same chassis, 40bhp engine and associated running gear, with the only major difference being that the Rialto's rear axle was borne by single-leaf rear springs. With the change of power at Tamworth as a result of the arrival of the Nash Group, Tom Karen's Ogle Designs Ltd had been discarded as Reliant's chief styling consultancy in favour of the Worthing-based IAD (International Automotive Design) UK Ltd and so the new Rialto did at least have a new body-shell to look at. IAD embraced an angular philosophy with frontal styling consisting of a sloping bonnet with a large, full-width black plastic radiator grille that, combined with square headlights, gave the Rialto an appearance similar to that of the contemporary Austin Mini-Metro. The front bumper was also deeper and extended the full length of the front side-panels, whilst the passenger doors were carried over from the Robin with no modifications. At the rear, the saloon was the most visually altered in the range with a square profile and, for the first time since 1973, a separate boot compartment, with a downward hinging lid, was to be found. Elsewhere, the Rialto estate and van closely followed the outgoing Robin models in terms of rear styling except for a deeper rear bumper matching the frontal styling. Inside all three new models, the general specification and layout were again hardly altered from that of the Robin, except for modern antennae controls for the lights, horn and windscreen wipers. Two versions of each Rialto model were offered: the basic model and the GLS, the latter being identifiable by its removable parcel shelf and separate sidelights amongst other detail refinements. The Rialto was an instant success, and just what Reliant needed to pull them back from the brink.

Opposite: A bold new style for a bold new decade as Reliant introduces the new wedge-shaped Rialto in October 1981. It was the age of the microchip and this was reflected in the choice of graphics for the new car's identifying logos, almost resembling the lettering style sometimes found on old 32-bit computer screen displays.

This early top-of-the-range Rialto GLS saloon shows off very well the sleek angular styling that enabled the required dramatic change of appearance from the outgoing and very curvy Robin whilst still retaining all the successful aspects of the Karen/Crosthwaite design.

Not only did the Rialto feature a fibreglass body, the chassis was also now galvanised for extra longevity. Reports suggest that some late Robins were also fitted with the galvanised chassis though it was primarily a feature introduced for the Rialto range. Eagle-eyed readers will note that this chassis is left-hand drive.

The Rialto's styling by IAD Ltd worked particularly well with the estate car model as this profile view amply demonstrates. As had been proved a few years earlier by the Robin models, the Rialto estate, with its useful extra load capacity, was to be the bestseller of the range throughout production.

Whilst at first glance the body of the Rialto looked very different from the outgoing Robin, it was produced in exactly the same way, with the main shell being laid up by hand. Cost-cutting directives were beginning to bite, however, and so the Rialto made use of the earlier model's doors. *David Poole*

This rare photo from 1981 shows a number of Rialto bodies being moulded prior to the official launch of the model on 13 January 1982. Also apparent from this image is Reliant's method of mating the bare body to its chassis and then mounting the whole thing onto trolley wheels for easy manoeuvrability. *David Poole*

The rear hatch window on the Robin was prone to leaking in heavy rain and so this may have prompted the designers of the Rialto to go for a drop down tailgate below the window. In principle it worked well though, unlike the hatch window on the Robin, it severely hampered the way the vehicle was loaded from the rear as items could be stacked no higher than the top of the door.

In 1984 the Rialto 2 range was unveiled. Although externally practically identical to the original Rialto, except for a slightly different radiator grille and a 'Rialto 2' badge, mechanically, for the first time since 1975, there was a new version of the 848cc engine. Known as the HT-E (High Torque-Economy) engine, torque had been increased by 7.3% to 49.5lb by raising compression ratios, revising camshaft profiles and alterations to the distributor and carburettor, which in turn gave a 14.3% reduction in engine speed, giving extra fuel economy. This engine was also the first Reliant unit to run on unleaded petrol and was readily identifiable by a yellow rocker box cover. Once again the Rialto 2 was offered as saloon, estate or van variants with each model available in either Standard or GLS form. In 1985, coinciding with the Reliant Motor Company's 50th anniversary celebrations, the 10,000th Rialto was produced. Unfortunately, behind the scenes, there was no cause for celebrations. The miners' strike in 1984/85 meant that sales of the Rialto were severely depressed and this hit many Reliant dealers hard, causing a number of them to go out of business. This all meant that Reliant was again in the red, making a loss of £649,000 for that year. As a result, in 1986, the entire range was reorganised, with the standard variants of both the saloon and estate models being discontinued. All van

RIALTO 2
more style... even MORE economy

The 1984 Rialto 2 range saw several modifications to the basic Rialto, not least a new High Torque-Economy (HT-E) engine, a higher ratio rear axle and improved creature comforts inside, including inertia-reel seatbelts for the first time in a Reliant three-wheeler.

Into the 1980s, sales of Reliant 5-cwt vans were constantly being outstripped by their passenger carrying counterparts, making this 1984 Reliant Rialto 2 van a rare sight indeed. Two years later, in 1986, the van model would be dropped from the range, ending 51 years of constant commercial vehicle production for Reliant.

A number of Rialto 2 estates captured outside the two Gates factory in 1985. Close examination of the photo reveals two Reliant employees drinking tea in the doorway to the building at the rear. One hopes it is an official tea-break or there will be hell to pay if their foreman catches them... *David Poole*

The 848cc HT-E engine as fitted to the Rialto 2 and identified by its yellow rocker cover. With increased engine toque the engine offered almost 74mpg at a constant 56mph and also provided the car with a slightly increased top speed.

models were also discontinued, leaving only the GLS saloon and estate in production, both of which were renamed as the Rialto SE range. Despite this severe pruning of the three-wheeler range, there was one new Rialto model within the new line-up of 1986, Reliant following the trends of the rest of the motor industry by announcing a three-door hatchback Rialto.

By the mid-1980s, the Reliant three-wheeler was being regarded by the industry and customers alike as a pretty average product in comparison with other vehicles on the market — a far cry from its heyday only a decade earlier. In an effort to combat this less than flattering general opinion, the Robin model name was resurrected during 1989 for the new luxury Reliant three-

Left: The Zoe Z/5000 series was an attempt by Zoe Motors Inc of the USA to introduce the Reliant Rialto to the American market. As with the UK, many American states classified a three-wheeler as a motorcycle, so exempting it from many safety standards applied to four wheelers. Alas, America was not interested, and very few cars were sold.

Below: For 1986 Zoe Motors Inc introduced the Z/3000ST version of the Reliant Rialto in which the rear axle and bodywork were considerably widened. Although extensively marketed, with both 'sedan/wagon' and 'panel van' variations offered, America once again displayed its total indifference and only six Z/3000ST prototypes were built, of which only two or three are known to exist today.

wheeler. Offered only as a saloon, the new Robin LX was mechanically identical to its Rialto SE stable mates and closely followed the Rialto SE hatchback in terms of styling at the rear. Yet it had been given its own personality at the front, primarily by the incorporation of headlights taken from the recently discontinued Ford Fiesta Mk II and a much smaller radiator grille. Although the glory days of the 1970s were long gone, Reliant nevertheless still had a very healthy order book at the turn of the 1990s, but events within the parent Nash Group were about drastically to overtake the Reliant three-wheeler.

Following a complicated and expensive 'reverse takeover' of a property business during 1988, Nash suffered badly when the bottom suddenly fell out of the housing market almost immediately afterwards, triggering a nationwide recession. Despite every effort, J. F. Nash Securities Limited was declared Bankrupt and the receivers

Such was the impact of the Robin name — or 'Robin Mk II' as it was also became known in later years by Reliant enthusiasts — that the Robin LX was reintroduced in 1989 on a redesigned vehicle using Ford Fiesta headlights and a new front grille. The Robin LX and, later, SLX models would replace the Rialto range by 1993.

Left: On 25 October 1990, the Nash Group and the Reliant Motor Company were declared bankrupt, with the pieces being picked up by Beans Industries Ltd. Following a short, sharp period of reorganisation, the autumn 1991 Reliant range now consisted of Robin LX saloon, Rialto SE hatchback and the surprise reintroduction of the 5-cwt Rialto van, a model last seen in 1986.

This particular 1990 Reliant Robin LX was driven from Tamworth to the North Cape of Norway and back in 2008 by one of the co-authors, Elvis Payne, and his brother, Geoff, covering 5,500 miles in 21 days; this, if nothing else, demonstrated the reliability of a Reliant three-wheeler.

Above: On 8 April 1993, Elvis Payne toured the Reliant premises. This was the assembly line at the time with just two vehicles on it. During that week, just 25 Robins were made with three of those cars bound for Austria — a far cry from the factory's heyday in the late 1960s and early 1970s when over 300 vehicles per week would be pouring from the lines.

Middle: Another view of the assembly line in April 1993. For a single vehicle to make its way from bare shell at one end of the assembly to completed car at the other took 15 man hours. Even with 58 years of assembling experience behind them, the Reliant three-wheeler was still very much a handmade product.

Left: The Two Gates paint shop recorded again during the April 1993 tour. Once the body parts for the Robin had been formed and combined into a single shell, the completed body was then sent to the paint shop to be sprayed. Each vehicle received three coats of paint with the choice derived from a chart of seven basic colours or seven optional colours available at that time.

were called in on 25 October 1990, forcing the Reliant Motor Company to cease trading as the knock-on effects rippled their way through the Nash concern's many subsidiaries. In January 1991, following intervention from Lord Stokes, the former Chairman of the vast British Leyland combine, the Reliant Motor Company was purchased by Beans Industries Ltd, which, in a previous incarnation back in the 1920s, had been a prominent motor manufacturer in its own right, but had concentrated on general engineering work in later years. This work had included, since the late 1980s, manufacturing the 848cc engine on behalf of Reliant. Reliant vehicle production restarted under Bean ownership during autumn 1991. The old range had been reduced, consisting only of the Rialto SE saloon and estate as well as the Robin LX, whilst the Rialto SE hatchback had been discarded, but a surprise return to the range was made by the Rialto van, a model last seen in 1986. In 1993 the LE Ninety Three 'special' was introduced, to celebrate 40 years of Reliant passenger vehicle production between 1953 and 1993. Internally, the model was no different to any other Robin, externally colour flashes were applied to the sills in either blue with yellow or red with brown on white bodywork with the words 'Ninety Three' just above the passenger (near) side headlight. During September 1993, the remaining members of the Rialto range were discontinued, leaving the Robin LX as the sole Reliant three-wheeler in production. Then, just as things looked to have settled down again at last for the Reliant Motor Company, history repeated itself in November 1994 with cash flow problems forcing the Reliant company to close its doors once more, this time dragging Beans Industries Ltd into receivership alongside it. Reliant was then acquired by Avonex Group Ltd on 16 January 1995, led by Peter Hall and, as the year marked the company's 60th anniversary, a new limited edition model was released called the Diamond Robin. Finished in pearlescent diamond white with a grey leather seats the Diamond Robin also featured a stereo radio /cassette with a CD socket.

The Robin 'LE Ninety Three' built in 1993 to commemorate 40 years of passenger vehicle production from 1953 to 1993. *Alan Gold*

Peter Hall and the Avonex Group also had plans to put the Bond Bug back into production at this time, but a quick glance at the Reliant Company inventory revealed that the entire Bond package, consisting of name, moulds and production rights, had been sold by the Official Receivers in 1990 for 'just thousands' to Mike and Gary Webster of Braishfield, Hampshire, who had been using the moulds to produce the four-wheeled WMC Bug ever since. In order to proceed with their new Bug idea, the Avonex Group found itself having to negotiate with the Websters. As a result certain aspects of the design were eventually sold back to the Reliant Motor Company. In mid-1995 Peter Hall contacted Tom Karen, the Bug's original designer, and commissioned him to help bring the Bug into the 1990s, the result of which was the 'Sprint'. With more than a passing hint of familiarity to the original Bug, the Sprint was a much curvier vehicle with frog eyed headlights, a sunroof and flared wheel arches to the rear. Finished in bright yellow, the Sprint was due to be launched on 2 April 1996 but, before this could happen, Reliant once more went into receivership, on 22 December 1995, and the project was shelved.In a way, the development costs of the Sprint, and several other stillborn projects, were partly to blame, as was the Avonex Group's policy of increasing staff numbers before being able to justify such increases with vehicle sales. Indeed, not one single entirely brand-new car was ever produced during the entire 12 months of the Avonex tenancy, for although 40 cars in total left the Two Gates works between January and April, and climbed to 80 per month by November, every Avonex-produced car was just the completion of a part-assembled vehicle left behind from the Bean's crash of 1994. Indeed, there was in fact very little remaining at Two Gates with which to build any completely new cars, for the manufacture of engines, drive trains and chassis had been progressively subcontracted to outside suppliers throughout the late 1980s and early 1990s, the Two Gates works acting as little more than an assembly line. With the outside suppliers refusing to play the game any longer, this really did look like the end of the road for the Reliant marque...

The Sprint was an attempt in 1995 by the Avonex Group to revamp the Bond Bug for the 1990s with Tom Karen being brought back to work on his original design. Unmistakably a Bug and significantly far enough advanced to have an official launch date set for 2 April 1996, the Sprint project became just one of the casualties when the company crashed once more into receivership in December 1995.
Mark Cropper

RELIANT MOTORS LTD

DIAMOND ROBIN

The Robin Pedigree

The Diamond Robin has a character all of its own. Luxurious and fun to drive, it is also extremely reliable and very cost effective to run.

The steel chassis is built for strength and fully galvanised for a long life. The reinforced glass fibre body has proven to be tough and highly durable.

The Diamond Robin may be small and unassuming but it's big enough to deliver a top speed in excess of the legal limit and safely carry four persons.

Powered by the latest version of the renowned Reliant 848cc alloy engine. Built in Tamworth, this engine has served customers around the world for decades. Constant quality control and recent improvements ensure that you can expect impressive fuel economy.

The Diamond Robin is equally at home touring the country side or running around town. It is easily manoeuvred and has plenty of space to carry the shopping.

The Diamond Robin is hand built with pride. Servicing is quick and efficient, spare parts are inexpensive. As rust is not a problem, a regularly serviced engine will ensure the Diamond Robin gives you many years of low cost motoring.

Diamond Robin 60th Anniversary Special Edition

Our top of the range Robin, fully featured, to celebrate 60 years of motor manufacturing an achievement we are very proud of.

Finished in beautiful Pearlescent Diamond White and based on the Robin hatchback. This special edition also offers; luxury grey leather seating, stereo radio/ cassette (with CD socket), rear washer/wiper, stylish front driving lights and heated rear window all as standard.

By January 1995, Reliant was once more bankrupt with the reins of command now passing to the Avonex Group. To promote sales, Avonex introduced the special edition 'Diamond' Robin to celebrate the 60th anniversary of the Reliant company. Finished in pearlescent white with grey leather trim, the mechanical specification was otherwise unchanged.

The Jonathan Heynes Era: 1996-1998

*At the eleventh hour, the Reliant Motor Company was saved from oblivion for the third time in five years during March 1996 when it was purchased by a consortium led by Jonathan Heynes, son of William Heynes, the Jaguar car company's chief engine designer. We consider ourselves extremely fortunate in having received this exclusive chapter, penned by Jonathan Heynes himself in which he recounts his time with Reliant. **EP & SC***

In late 1994 Reliant was purchased from receivers of Beans Industries by Avonex Ltd an engineering company without previous automobile experience. Avonex recommenced production of the Robin models in January 1995 and also continued with the Scimitar Sabre in limited production. Avonex was controlled by a well-known businessman Peter Hall, who had a great passion and belief to see Reliant salvaged and turned around into a profitable business in a brief period. Regretfully financial difficulties became apparent after six months. Finance for cars was provided by a contracted international Finance House in London. This finance transaction of finished cars allowed the company to continue. However, demands from suppliers were gathering pace. In October 1995 funds to pay suppliers and work force became more critical, and, as can be imagined the difficulties, although confidential at the time, resulted in rumours amongst the supplier network beginning to take hold. In December the London Finance group pulled out and, with non-supply of key components, the company, which was still controlled by Avonex, had no option than to call in Administrators — Finn Associates.

Finn Associates, at an early stage in December, decided to find a buyer for the whole of Reliant as a going concern. The workforce was reduced to 12 from 95, with limited production to complete partly built cars. However, the Administrators, in order to enable partly finished cars to be completed, were compelled to sell off some key parts to continue cash flow into the production business. In January 1996 the problems at Reliant were major news stories and I made an approach to the Administrators early that month. I had previously had a 25-year career at Jaguar and held senior positions that provided an all-round knowledge of the auto industry and suppliers. It was clear that the Reliant Company was struggling to continue and the premises in a short period had deteriorated. However, the spirit of the remaining work force remained high and enthusiastic. Also dealers reviewed were also confident of future sales. I visited the Tamworth site on about 20 occasions over the next two months, researching and reviewing what was required to take over and build Reliant back into a good profitable car company.

The significant key point was to ensure supply of components could be continued. This was a major task as Reliant was the sole remaining UK car company producing the complete car on one site, encompassing engine, gearbox, axle, body and paint. The supplier base numbered some 440 companies. This must be taken in context with, for example, Land Rover that, at the time, had 280 suppliers! I ensured key personnel would be able to return: Maurice Green, Works Director; Brian Benton, Production Superintendent; Alan Hunt, Machine Shop Foreman; Roger Dean, IT and administration; Mick Hilton, Service Manager; and, Sid Gray, Car Production Foreman as well as many others who all showed great strength of character. Due diligence with the key suppliers was carried out by myself and only two suppliers felt they would not be able to continue. I ensured, as part of the purchase, that the tooling at suppliers was owned by Reliant. However, all suppliers required cash up front prior to supplies being delivered without exception.

Obtaining finance and cash flow was of course paramount. I decided to arrange a meeting with the London Finance House, who had lost about £250,000 during the Avonex period. There were 28 cars to complete at Tamworth and I realised that, if I completed these cars, which were technically the property of the Finance House, then the Finance House would finance the completion! This deal was successfully negotiated and £100,000 cash was injected into the company within the first four weeks. Securing the rental agreement from the Tamworth site landlord was anticipated to be a difficulty. However, I think my pleading to be reasonable paid off, and we entered a five-year contract at £80,000 per year payable quarterly. Importantly I negotiated an option break clause at two years. This would have allowed us either to purchase the site, which had vast housing potential, or to vacate without penalty. This was an important key moment prior to agreeing the company purchase.

During my due diligence I was approached by Staffordshire Business Link; it had a proposal that was considered and followed up. The proposal was for Reliant to be purchased in conjunction with Fletcher Speedboats in Burntwood, Staffordshire. The joint use of fibreglass was the reasoning for a combined production facility. The Fletcher's site, close to the then proposed M6 toll road, was approximately five acres with modern facilities. Fletcher was owned as a subsidiary of Hornby Group PLC, the model railway specialists. Discussions with Hornby took place. The purchase price was approximately, after my negotiation, £640,000. However, the deal was not concluded. I decided to concentrate on Reliant solely. However, I was aware of another bidder for Fletcher Speedboats. Strategic moves were being made to assure local Staffordshire employment. During Administration eight serious purchase enquiries were received by Finn Associates, two of which came from overseas.

Enquiry number one was from an off-shore company called Burton West Ltd. Little was known about this company, although the 'buyers' were put in touch with me and it became evident the company was a large Indian group, San Engineering & Locomotive Co Ltd, manufacturers of locomotive engines in Bangalore. San had recently purchased the Indian intellectual property rights to the Dolphin-Reliant power train, which previously had been sold to the Indian company by Beans Industries. Therefore, San had the commercial rights to produce Reliant power trains in India. San wished to manufacture a small sports car in India, with the Reliant power train. They also wished to purchase Reliant Tamworth. The administrators put us in touch and we decided on a 50/50 purchase with myself being sole director as San required the Tamworth business to continue and flourish. Purchase of Reliant continued, with our London solicitors Marriott A Harrison detailing and completing matters.

Enquiry number two, in conjunction with the UK deal, the Administrators, Finn Associates, were working closely with an overseas buyer who became very prominent. This overseas company was Indonesian-controlled through a UK agent. Indonesian legislation allowed huge import duty benefits for importing vehicles if from an Indonesian-controlled company. Therefore, the purchase of Reliant was an opportunistic chance to secure rights for an Indonesian company. The Administrators, therefore, sold the overseas intellectual property rights to the Indonesian company, *and* to the UK and Indian manufacturing, as well as the brand name to my consortium. In effect Reliant was sold twice! We had Indonesian representatives at Reliant for a 90-day contracted period where blueprint drawing copies were made of the power train designs. To this day, I remain unsure what happened to this project. This overseas involvement made no difference to the UK operation.

During the last week of completion, the Administrators received an offer from Glen Investments Jersey, and I spoke directly with Kevin Leech, who was a highly successful businessman with some 60 UK companies in his portfolio. There was no doubt that, had he wished, he was able to purchase Reliant outright in conjunction with Fletcher in Burntwood. However, he wanted someone to take control and run the business with little interference. He chose me, and purchase negotiations continued. Consulting with San in India, I formed the opinion the purchase should be split three ways. This Kevin Leech agreed and, by the end of the week, we had a done deal signed and sealed by me in very expensive solicitors' offices on the Thames embankment, London. I was the owner of a car company!

On my way back to the Midlands, I was contacted by the BBC and asked to come over to their studio and provide input into the deal. This I did with a certain amount of 'gusto' at 9pm that night. I listened to 'my news story' at 10pm on the way back up the M1! I arranged to be at Tamworth at 9am Easter Saturday. Surprisingly, the local Midlands news cameras were awaiting me at the gatehouse, where I was handed the keys by the security guard. So again we hit the news. On the basis that all publicity is good publicity we enjoyed the moment! On arrival we had one working telephone in the gatehouse. I started work by calling dealers to let them know Reliant was back, but they knew this from the news coverage and by the end of the day we had received 22 car orders! I called Kevin Leech, who was pretty impressed and exclaimed 'ere lad we will pay for the company in a month at this rate!'

Roger Dean and Maurice Green quickly started reviewing what the Administrators had left us and, within the first week, we had good knowledge of our supplier position and stock of parts. For example, during administration, parts had been sold or had disappeared with the result that we had no pistons. The piston supplier would not manufacture without cash up front for 100 sets. This pattern of zero supply without cash payments went on mostly for the first six months. The cash injection, mentioned previously, from the finance company was a bold and good move on our part. With car production starting up and with completion of cars, cash began to flow.

During due diligence we were alerted that the engine-casting supplier could prove to be reluctant to supply. We placed an order for 100 engine-casting sets. This was refused and was followed up with a phone call stating Reliant did not own the tooling, the supplier having claimed a lien on the tooling. This came as a bombshell. The tooling, we later found out, had been illegally purchased by one of the interested parties in the sell-off. We had no option but to get an urgent court hearing at the Supreme Court in London to overthrow the deal that had been 'incorrectly completed' by the casting supplier. Due to this, the Judge ordered the 100 sets of castings to be manufactured at speed. The cost of the Court case was a six-figure sum, which we could not reclaim as the casting company later went into liquidation due to its court costs! This, fortunately, was the only significant delay in production restarting but did result in a huge drain on shareholder funds.

We were contacted within days of the purchase by the BBC. The request was for an episode within the 10-part business programme *Trouble At The Top*. The proposal was for a BBC camera crew to be within Reliant for six months during start up. We were at first reluctant in view of the previously detailed court case; however, after considerable urging by my friends, we gave the go-ahead. The Court case remained confidential within the programme for legal reasons. This turned out to be a very significant turning point; the 45-minute programme was shown in prime time and drew a huge audience. This was probably uniquely for Reliant and the fondness of Del Boy, and it was a huge success. Importantly, after the film was shown prior to Christmas 1996, we gained higher morale and suppliers provided credit terms. Sales increased and we were having three months of forward orders from our dealers.

By week six we had completed the finance company cars, and previously ordered cars were in production. Things were looking bright and Brian Benton was hiring back former employees. Suppliers were coming on side and orders were building up. By week 12 we had completed 60 cars and we had an order bank of eight weeks. Production was maintained on the original tooling and machines; however, age was beginning to tell. We set about reviewing a new fibreglass process by spraying fibreglass rather than the hand method of layering. With this in mind we started to review a new look Robin. Engine and gearbox production was a problem and we commenced obtaining major components from San India, namely crankshafts, con rods, pistons, distributors and carburettors. The total work force by December 1997 stood at 105 and, by April 1998, we had produced 1,365 Robins and derivatives in a 24-month period from start up. We were very proud of this achievement. We continued to sell engines to Angus Fire, a major customer for their lightweight fire pump, still operated to this day in some Commonwealth countries.

Jonathan Heynes (centre) and his wife Samantha (opposite on the right) seen with the Reliant work force in 1997. At this time, two Robin vans had been sold to the US Embassy in London and a special dark — Bentley Green — van with wood veneer interior had also been made for Princess Anne. This was personally delivered by Jonathan Heynes to Gatcombe Park. *Jonathan Heynes*

After some experimental thoughts on larger Reliant vehicles, we concentrated on the 850cc models and how we could improve the range within our model parts bin. The first move was rapidly to introduce quality engineering into the product. Components that were known to cause problems, such as widow lifts, door sealing and cooling, were quickly modified. With the likelihood of progressing to new Resin Injected Moulding (RIM) techniques, we decided to restyle the exterior of the Robin as new body tooling would be required. With assistance of a graduate from the renowned Coventry School for Design, several new shapes were viewed. A more flowing rounded shape was chosen by me with Corsa supplied headlamps to reduce tooling cost. We were extremely pleased with the shape, which I felt to be modern yet in keeping for Robin customers. We also decided to evaluate diesel for four-wheel future cars, and we prepared a prototype diesel three-cylinder Lombardini-engined car. This would have been satisfactory for emissions and provided outstanding economy in a lightweight body. This prototype was shown to all the dealers with a positive response within the motorcycle licence sector framework. We also evaluated a Kubota diesel, which was noisier.

During this rather extensive engineering programme, on a very tight budget, we decided to produce a four-wheel Bond Bug. A full prototype was completed and showed much promise. We managed to obtain much media positive comment. Also we manufactured two long-wheelbase chassis cab prototypes. This model had potential, particularly had we produced the four-wheel version. One of the prototypes was despatched to Land's End for commercial use. In addition looking towards the future, we sold five glider cars without engines to a company in Seattle, USA, for conversion to electric motor drive. I visited this company and drove an Electric Robin through Seattle. I remain unsure what happened to that project. With electrical propulsion in mind, we prepared an electrically-driven Robin at Tamworth, but with the motor driving through a standard gearbox and clutch. We later decided to fit a constant-velocity-transmission (CVT) drive. During this period we were advised by Bob Knight, formerly Technical Director of Jaguar. As readers will now realise we had an ambitious programme for new model launches in 1999-2000, being:

■ **Restyled** — Robin with existing 850 engine saloon, van, pick-up, long wheelbase versions;

■ **New** — Kitten four-wheel with 850cc EFI MPI engine or with Lombardini Diesel option;

■ **New** — Bond Bug four-wheel with 850cc EFI MPI engine closed top (Targa) and open Clubman versions;

■ **New** — small Scimitar 1,000cc sports roadster.

A number of Robin van and saloon shells await to be called to the assembly line in 1998. In the lower right hand corner a Reliant TW9 cab is also visible. *Thomas Touw*

The Avonex Group only lasted a year and, in March 1996, Reliant passed into the hands of Jonathan Heynes. Under his guidance, Reliant focused more attention upon its commercial vehicle range with the reintroduction of the 'Supervan' in 1996, now based upon the Robin LX. With a capacity of 40cu ft, Reliant hoped that, once again, the Supervan would find favour with both large and small companies.

Another commercial model revived by Heynes was an October 1995 Avonex prototype pick-up truck based upon the Rialto. Originally known as the '850 Pick-up', the name was swiftly changed in 1996 to 'Giant', with the lowest model in the new range being named the 'Giant L' and featuring Rialto styling with drop-down tailgate at the rear

This 1999 Giant SLX is higher up the 'Giant' range and so is based on the Robin Mk II body. With a wider loading area than the base-model Giant L, the Giant SLX was wide enough to carry a Euro-pallet. *Kerry Croxton*

Prior to the purchase, Unipart had been contracted by Beans Industries to market and control all spare parts. With administration in place, I contested the previous contract was void, and I was successful in purchasing, with Glen Investments, the complete Unipart stock held in warehousing at Long Marston. The stock was valued at £250,000 and I was pleased to report a bargain buy to Kevin Leech. He thought this was wonderful news. This stock, together with production parts coming on stream, realised the potential of the high margins to be gained on parts sales. I came up with the idea of 'PartsWorld' as a spares brand. I then advertised for a Parts Manager, and we hired Bruce Morris, who worked in a similar role at Carbodies London Taxis. This was again a significant moment as we had a second cash-flow stream, which was much needed to fund our new model proposals.

We were fortunate to have an established Reliant dealership chain. The loyalty of the dealers was immense, particularly when ordering and paying for cars on delivery. Customer loyalty to the Reliant brand was huge and the Reliant Owners Clubs in regional areas were a great boost to us back at the factory. We attended rallies and assisted where possible on a low budget. The Reliant Owners Club is flourishing to this day; long may it continue. Bruce Morris was promoted to Sales and Parts Director, and drove sales upwards. By December 1997 we were building 24 Robins a week. The workforces continued to be people of 'true grit' and were flexible in all types of work without question.

I have previously described the three-way split on the initial purchase in March 1996. It was arranged that the three shareholders would place working cash funds into the company as cash flow demanded during the first year in equal amounts by ratio of shares. This programme worked well. After the first year, Glen Investments, which had also purchased Fletcher Speedboats in Burntwood, requested a full move from Tamworth to their site, which had certainly enough space. They requested a new lease contract that provided the rent to Fletcher. The move would be costly and lose several weeks of production. My Indian partners felt unsure about the move and believed we should stay at Tamworth. This caused a ripple in shareholder relations. I had already moved entirely the newly acquired parts stock to Burntwood and I was making the plans to move production lock, stock and barrel. However, the tenancy agreement with the Tamworth landlord meant we could be locked into a further three years if we did not hurry. I needed to plan the move prior to the tenancy break clause at two years' occupancy. It was a difficult situation as my other two shareholders had differing approaches. We also had the option to purchase, for £800,000, the Tamworth site, which would have been a valuable potential housing site. Glen Investments was quite keen for this to happen; however, the funds needed would have been more difficult to obtain.

During this period we understood the backers of San Engineering in India — Burton West Ltd — were concerned about the move as they felt their share was

Unlike production Giants, this particular example is an experimental prototype fitted with a three-cylinder Kubota diesel engine. It never reached production. *Kerry Croxton*

Here we see two vehicles Reliant described as 'chassis cabs' at Two Gates in 1998 prior to receiving their rear bodywork. This view illustrates well the enclosed cabs and exposed chassis at the rear. *Kerry Croxton*

The long-wheel-based 'Chassis cab', with a drop-side loading area, did not reach production, however, due to legislation on braking weights. *Jonathan Heynes*

Jonathan Heynes also continued with the theme of introducing special editions to keep the public interested in the Reliant three-wheeler, announcing the 'Racing Green' Robin in December 1996. As the name suggests, this particular special was finished in metallic British Racing Green.

48

A number of Robin bodies are seen awaiting assembly after being painted in 1998. *David Poole*

being diluted. Also the plans to purchase components from San, due in the main to teething quality issues, was not proceeding with the pace the Indian shareholder wanted. At this time Burton West Ltd negotiated for Glen investments Jersey Ltd to purchase its share and investment to date. In short, Kevin Leech bought out the Indian shareholder following a brief exchange, which resulted in control of Reliant passing to Kevin Leech. With full control Kevin Leech appointed his senior accountant, Alan Sutton, to oversee Glen Investments' UK businesses. These now totalled, I believe, 64 ventures including Reliant. All throughout the period I had been the sole Director and sole authorised bank signature authority. In the second quarter of 1997 we had achieved a profit and the future looked promising. I was then requested to stop further engineering work and to abandon the projects mentioned previously. This was hugely disappointing since, with fairly limited funding, we had achieved much in less than two years. Glen Investments wanted me to move production to Fletcher's site immediately. For me to remain in control would have been more difficult as Glen Investments was requesting a business restructure, possibly in the order of £4m with a ratio raised by myself. This would have been not viable commercially.

It later became quite apparent Kevin Leech required full control. He personally requested I take the position as Chairman on a good contract of three years. However, I decided to sell my share ratio to Leech and to obtain all my investment and finance input over two years and a very satisfactory financial settlement. Not the end I had anticipated; however, the Government had legislated for compact four-wheel cars — quadricycles — to be sold in the UK and it was fairly obvious the long life of the Reliant three-wheeler had reached a final plateau. The Tamworth plant was quickly closed within the tenancy break clause I have previously mentioned and the production transferred to Fletcher's site. The site was developed for housing. The new Robin shape — nicknamed 'Teardrop' by the dealers — which I approved and signed off, continued and was successfully launched at the end of 1998 from Fletcher at Burntwood. In 1999 I became the sole importer for Microcar, a compact four-wheel competitor to Robin.

Jonathan Heynes,
Stratford-on-Avon, July 2011

One of the proposed concepts for the Robin Mk III featuring a nose with BMW ZKW front lights and Land Rover indicators. *Jonathan Heynes*

The concept for the Robin Mk III using Vauxhall Corsa headlights.This actual design was signed off for production in January 1998. *Jonathan Heynes*

The rear of the Robin Mk III concept using Rover 100 tail-lights. *Jonathan Heynes*

From Burntwood to Sudbury: 1999-2002

With Kevin Leech now in full charge, sweeping changes were about to hit the Reliant company. The company name was changed from 'Reliant Motor Company Ltd' to 'Reliant Cars Ltd', and the announcement was made that the historic, but somewhat neglected, Two Gates plant was to be vacated during January 1999 in favour of a brand-new £1,750.000 purpose-built factory at the premises of Fletcher Speedboats in Burntwood, 15 miles from Tamworth. The Two Gates site was then demolished to make way for the long-mooted housing estate. Before the move took place, the last few months of 1998 saw Reliant producing a commemorative edition Reliant Robin that marked the last 50 vehicles made at the Tamworth plant. Each one contained a commemorative plaque on the dashboard that stated: 'Reliant Cars Ltd. Reliant Robin Commemorative Edition. No. (#). Built to commemorate the last 50 cars to be built at the Two Gates Factory, in Tamworth, Staffordshire'.

To mark the last 50 vehicles to be built at the Tamworth factory, the 1998 Reliant Robin Commemorative edition was announced. Each car was individually numbered from one to 50, and all were finished in yellow.

After 65 years of production and after once spreading across both sides of the A5, the latter years saw Reliant shrink drastically with production being contained in just a few buildings on the north side of the A5 at Tamworth. This view from 1998 was one that had greeted many Tamworthians day in and day out. *Martin North*

The final remnants of the Two Gates plant are demolished with the old company logo, a proud survivor of the late 1960s, still adorning the building to the very end. A year later and this area would be swallowed up by a housing estate aptly named Scimitar Park. *Martin North*

As Jonathan Heynes has discussed in the previous chapter, a new restyled Reliant Robin was standing by in the pipeline and this was unveiled in March 1999 as the Reliant Robin 3. Again built upon the same chassis and mechanics that could be traced back to 1973 and 1975 respectively, the new body-shell had brought the Reliant three-wheeler firmly back into the modern world and was again offered in either LX, SLX, B.R.G or Royale form, with prices ranging between £8,137.00 for the LX, £8,459.00 for the SLX and £9,654.00 for the B.R.G or Royale. Sadly, by the turn of the 21st century, the Reliant three-wheeler was now really only selling to the loyal but ever-decreasing band of die-hard Reliant drivers who would not entertain the thought of driving any other type of car, rather than to the economy-minded masses which had served the company so well in earlier years. Advances in the four-wheel car industry had left the Reliant three-wheeler lagging behind in many aspects and even the Reliant's staple selling point of useful fuel economy had been eroded as many other cars, both large and small, on the market were now more than capable of matching the Reliant in those terms. In addition, the Reliant also scored badly in the comfort stakes and, when all was said and done, it was the high purchase price that plagued the Robin 3 from the outset. This was an Achilles' Heel that had always set the Reliant three-wheeler at a disadvantage against its competition throughout its long history. In 1999, the £10,000 cost of an 848cc Robin 3 Royale was the equivalent of almost any 1,100cc to 1,500cc five-door hatchback on the market, and most prospective purchasers did indeed end up choosing the larger car.

On 26 September 2000, Leech and Reliant Cars Ltd finally threw in the towel and announced that all vehicle production was to end during December 2000. Reliant dealers were informed that the deadline for all orders was 31 November 2000. At this point in time the Reliant company was employing 60 staff on manufacturing, engineering spares and sales. Thereafter, the company would concentrate all future

The Reliant Cars Ltd stand at the 2000 British Motor Show caused a few raised eyebrows as there wasn't a single Reliant vehicle on display. Instead there were numerous examples of the Italian three-wheeled 50cc Piaggio 'Ape' trucks for which Reliant had recently gained an import licence.

The Robin Union Jack is a preproduction Robin Mk III belonging to Kevin Leech. It is pictured here whilst on the 'Land's End to John O'Groats and back again campaign' for Cancer Research in 2008. *Kerry Croxton*

A 2000 van version of the Robin Mk 3, a model made in very limited numbers. Unlike vans of old, this van used the same body as the saloon version except that it had no rear windows.

The 2000 Robin SLX saloon was one of the Reliant three-wheeler models to take Reliant into the new millennium. An amazing feat in itself given how many three-wheeler manufacturers had fallen by the wayside during Reliant's existence.

efforts on the UK sales of Piaggio and Ligier vehicles from France, for which Reliant had been appointed import agents during 1999. In line with motor industry tradition, the Reliant three-wheeler was to be given a final fling in the form of a special 'limited edition'. Named the Robin 65, painted in gold and limited to just 65 examples, this limited edition had a walnut dashboard, leather upholstery, alloy wheels, stainless steel exhaust, chrome door handles, special paint finish, driving lamps, white instrument pack and RDS radio/cassette all as standard within a price tag of £10,000. Each vehicle had a numbered plaque that was to be engraved with the original owner's name. The final Reliant Robin 65 rolled off the production line on 14 February 2001 and was presented to its new owner by *The Sun* newspaper following a nationwide competition to win this last Reliant. With this vehicle, many felt the Reliant three-wheeler had at least reached the end of a rocky road. But the story was not quite over yet...

After Reliant announced in 2000 that it was no longer to make three-wheelers, it carried on producing the Robin LX, SLX, and the B.R.G and Royale — as pictured here — models during the run down.

For one man, Les Collier of B&N Plastics Ltd, of Sudbury, Suffolk, a world without a Reliant three-wheeler was unthinkable and so he approached Reliant Cars Ltd with a view to purchasing the production rights. The company was more than happy to oblige Collier and, by March 2001, announcements were being circulated that the Robin was to return to the market under the new name of Robin BN-1. Reliant Cars Ltd was still to produce the rolling chassis and 848cc engine at Burntwood, whence they were dispatched to the B&N Plastics' factory in Suffolk. The luxurious Robin 65 model produced by Reliant was used by B&N Plastics as a base model to which a number of improvements were made to distinguish the Robin BN-1. A lightly modified gearbox and rear axle were fitted, followed by the bodyshell, which was entirely the product of B&N Plastics. Although outwardly identical to the genuine Burntwood article, B&N Plastics Ltd made several alterations inside their

The final Reliant: the Robin 65, built to mark the 65th anniversary of the foundation of the Reliant Motor Company, also marked the end of vehicle production in Staffordshire. As befitted the name, 65 examples were produced with the last car leaving the factory on 14 February 2001.

Robin BN-1 with a brand-new dashboard design for the first time since 1973, along with a wider rear seat, increased sound proofing, new door cards and a sunroof fitted as standard equipment. The first production model was finished in silver and completed in June 2001 and was kept as a test vehicle.

Three Robin BN-1s were unveiled to the public in a blaze of glory on 12 July 2001 at Grays of Thrapston, Northamptonshire, with the Robin BN-1 being priced at £9,995. Along with the BN-1 details of a further variant were released: the Robin BN-2, which was fitted with electric windows as standard and finished in a 'light-reactive' paint that changed colour when seen from different viewpoints. The Robin BN-2 had a price tag of £10,800. Much was expected from the new Robin BN-1 and interest in both that and the Robin BN-2 was such that, by the launch date, B&N Plastics had received 132 orders. B&N Plastics Ltd planned a limited production of 250 vehicles a year, including a projected electric-powered Robin that would have a range of 50 miles between charges and a top speed of 50-55mph. However, only very limited numbers of Robin BN-1s were actually dispatched to dealers in early

A rare view inside the B&N Plastics' workshop at Sudbury in 2001, showing the on-going construction of the very first Robin BN-1 following the company's acquisition of the production licence after Reliant closed.

A number of chasses fitted with full running gear at B&N Plastics in Suffolk having been assembled by Reliant at its new factory in Cannock

The plush interior of the Robin BN-1 was totally redesigned with a new dashboard, door skins, centre console and leather seats as standard. This was the first time the interior had received a major change since the original Robin in 1973.

2002 when B&N Plastics was forced to halt the production lines. Reports in the *East Anglian Daily Times* indicated that the new Robin did not meet Government safety regulations as the model did not comply with new Driver and Vehicle Licensing Centre guidelines. Therefore, the Certificate of Modification proving safety was not in place, which effectively rendered it illegal to sell the car until required modifications had been done, at great expense, time and effort. Les Collier and his company worked solidly for six months to attempt to make the Robin BN-1 meet the required standards, but to no avail. In October 2002 B&N Plastics Ltd announced that all production had been suspended for an 'indefinite period'. In total, it is believed, just 20 vehicles were manufactured: 15 Robin BN-1s and five Robin BN-2s.

Collier and B&N Plastics Ltd are still determined to relaunch the Robin BN-1 though, at the time of this 'Nostalgia Road' book being written, no more Reliant three-wheelers have been produced, from either Burntwood or Sudbury. An incarnation of the Reliant Company still remains operational in Cannock, Staffordshire, under Kevin Leech, though now trading as 'Reliant PartsWorld Limited', offering spare parts and reconditioned engines for Reliant vehicles. The factory at Two Gates was demolished in 1999 and a housing estate sprung up in its place. With a nod to its heritage, this

Les Collier talks to Anglia Television at the launch of the Robin BN-1, an event that created a great deal of interest amongst the media with the story appearing in numerous newspapers as well as on television and radio.

In grand total, B&N Plastics is thought to have produced around 20 cars. The second-produced Robin BN-1 is seen here; its date of registration is 13 February 2002, exactly a year to the day after the Burntwood production line closed.

estate is called Scimitar Park. The main entrance road is named after Reliant's founder, as Tom Williams Way, and three streets are called after Reliant vehicles with Regal Close, Robin Close and Fox Close. The fibreglass moulding plant at Kettlebrook was also demolished, during the first decade of the 21st century, to give way to another housing estate, though the premises at Shenstone continue to exist — the last surviving tangible part in the Tamworth area of the Reliant legacy. And here, the story must end, but not the legend, for that will remain for as long as there are examples of the Reliant three-wheeler in all its many and varied forms still to be seen upon the roads of the world. Long may they continue!

This sales brochure for the Robin BN-2 was collected at the official launch of the Robin BN range at Grays of Thrapston on 12 July 2001. Loaded with extras and finished in a 'light-reactive' paint, around five Robin BN-2s are believed to have been manufactured.

Opposite: Although the Two Gates Reliant factory is little more than a memory, Reliant vehicles of all shapes and sizes continue to line the streets of Tamworth at the annual Reliant Gathering held as part of the town's Heritage /Festival Weekend every September.

The last Robin of all: this particular 2009 Robin BN-1, with the second-highest known chassis number, was a part-finished car left over from B&N Plastics following its decision to halt production in October 2002. In 2008 it was purchased by Eddie Kelly of Northern Ireland, who undertook the task of completing its build, for all parts used had to be brand-new and authentic in order for the car to retain its 'new' status and thus gain a current registration number, not easy when so many specialist items were missing. After a titanic struggle with the Irish licensing authorities, it finally received its long-coveted registration number on 29 April 2009. It stands today as the last Reliant three-wheeler to be registered as a brand-new car, some seven years after the end of production. *Eddie Kelly*

Index